LEOPARD

Fashion's Most Powerful Print

Hilary Alexander

LEOPARD

Fashion's Most Powerful Print

Hilary Alexander

Laurence King Publishing

'Leopard symbolizes power, glamour and something a little wild. All of these things are at the heart of Versace, which is why the print is at the heart of our house.

Why do we love to wear leopard-print? So we can feel closer to something that is breathtakingly beautiful, graceful and precious ... and just a little bit dangerous.'

Donatella Versace, Artistic Director & Vice President, Versace

Introduction

'I feel empowered when I wear leopard-print, which comes as no surprise when you consider that female leopards are the hunters of their pride!'

Claudia Schiffer, fashion icon

From pharaohs to popstars, from coronations to *Coronation Street,* from military to mass market, the lure of leopard has endured. It has featured in the history, culture and fashion of countless civilizations since the dawn of time. The leopard's speed, agility and ferocity, and the beauty of its distinctive rosettes, have captivated men and women from the Stone Age to the Digital Age. But it has been a fatal attraction. This mighty cat has been hunted, sacrificed, worshipped and worn; painted and paraded as a totem; enlisted as military regalia; and exploited as an exotic pet. Thankfully, increasing conservation efforts, along with designers such as Stella McCartney, who has built her brand on an anti-fur ethos, and Gucci's decision in 2017 to ban fur, have broadened the message that fake is fashion's best weapon – and leopard its finest example. This book is a celebration of that timeless print.

Wild Warrior

'The message of a leopard-print jumpsuit is clear: I am a huntress who delights in eating the offal of her prey.'

Simon Doonan, Creative Ambassador-at-Large, Barneys New York

From Neolithic cave paintings to Greek mythology and beyond, the image of the warrior – man or woman – has been linked to leopard. Leopard-skin was appropriated during the Napoleonic Wars, decorating uniforms and saddle-cloths of hussars and cavalry. Military bands, such as the Duke of Wellington's Pipes & Drums and the US Marines favoured leopard-skin in their uniforms. In early twentieth-century British society, fancy dress parties and tableaux were popular and much photographed. One of the most celebrated was Madame Yevonde's 'Goddesses' series of 1935, in which she photographed Diana Mitford as Venus draped in leopard, the Countess of Shrewsbury as Ariadne, and the racy Australian socialite Sheila Chisholm, then Lady Milbanke, as Penthesilea, the Amazonian warrior queen. The contemporary image of woman as warrior has been revisited on-screen and in television series such as *Xena: Warrior Princess* (1995–2001) and, more recently, *Game of Thrones*.

2 Naomi Campbell in leopard-print for Azzedine Alaïa Autumn/Winter 1991, Paris.

4 Donatella Versace in Versace at the 2017 Fashion Awards, London.

5 Claudia Schiffer in Anne Klein by Louis Dell'Olio. Photograph by Arthur Elgort for American *Vogue*, 1992.

6 A Native American-inspired shoot for French *Vogue*'s children's supplement

March 2013. Photograph by Andreas Sjödin.

10 Baroness Charlotte du Rietz of Hedensberg (1744–1820) dressed as Diana Goddess of the Hunt.

11 Into the wilds of haute couture: a leopard crepe georgette dress with gold-embroidered lace applique by John Galliano for Christian Dior Spring/Summer 1999 Haute Couture, Paris.

CATHARINA
VON SCHELL

MICHAEL
HINZ

LOVELY
FIERCE
SAVAGE
in COMBAT

LANA
QUEEN OF THE
AMAZONS
in TECHNICOLOR

2 Theseus and Hippolyte in combat on an Attic red figure lekythos, c. 420 BC, the Metropolitan Museum of Art, New York.

3 Cara Delevingne in Hedi Slimane for Saint Laurent Spring/Summer 2015, Paris.

4 *Lana: Queen of the Amazons*, 1964. The German film, starring Catharina von Schell, brought jungle chic to the silver screen.

15 Versace Spring/Summer 1992, Milan.

16 The traditional uniform of the Scottish Melrose Pipes and Drums Band.

17 Re-fashioning fur at Moschino Autumn/Winter 1998, Milan.

Capt. Sam. J. Richardson.

24 Wild clotheshorse and singer-songwriter Isaac Hayes, aged 28, in 1971. Hayes kept his closets crammed with crushed velvet pantsuits, leopard coats, fur suits and snakeskin boots.

25 Elizabeth Taylor as Cleopatra with on- and off-screen lover Richard Burton, who played Mark Antony, on set in Rome, 1962.

26–7 King of kings: the Omukama of Toro's happy family, Uganda, c.1920.

28 Prince Kekolokowina in a leopard-skin kaross, Eastern Cape, South Africa,

29 The Lady Milbanke as Penthesilea, Queen of the Amazons, for Madame Yevonde's 'Goddesses' series, inspired by the work of Surrealists Man Ray and Salvador Dalí, 1935.

Leopard Royalty

*'I've never met a leopard-print
I didn't like.'*

Diana Vreeland (1903–1989), fashion editor

Royalty and leopard fit together like hand in glove. The leopard has entranced royalty, real or assumed, for thousands of years. Marchesa Luisa Casati, the Belle Époque's 'fashion princess', had leopards as pets, was reportedly buried in leopard-print, and after her death, inspired designers such as John Galliano in his Dior years, Alexander McQueen and Karl Lagerfeld at Chanel. Leopard-print lover Anna Wintour, Editor-in-Chief of American *Vogue*, stalks the fashion pantheon as front-row queen, reigning supreme over the faux-leopard-clad 'Insta-royals' in crowns and coronets who populate the Dolce & Gabbana catwalks. The leopard also links royalty to screen queens and first ladies: Queen Elizabeth II, Princess Grace of Monaco, Elizabeth Taylor and Jackie Kennedy Onassis have all worn leopard-skin coats. Jackie's favourite designer, Oleg Cassini, was so horrified by the leopard-skin mania that he began using man-made fibres to produce fake fur. It was a concept that soap-opera queens like *Coronation Street*'s Bet Lynch happily embraced.

30 Anna Wintour seated alongside Grace Coddington at Sies Marjan Autumn/Winter 2016, New York.

32 Roberto Cavalli Spring/Summer 2012, Milan.

33 Kaia Gerber for Versace Spring/Summer 2018, Milan.

34 Sister act: The Atomic's Pyper America, Starlie Cheyenne and Daisy Clementine walk for Dolce & Gabbana Autumn/Winter 2018, Milan.

35 Queen Elizabeth II, Hollywood royalty Elizabeth Taylor and former First Lady Jacqueline Kennedy, in the 1960s.

36–7 Bet Lynch, played by Julie Goodyear, from cult soap opera *Coronation Street* in front of the Rovers Return Inn, 1995.

38 Slab stella that once belonged to Princess Nefertiabet, Giza, fourth dynasty, c.2530 BC. Ancient Egyptian women stencilled leopard rosettes onto cotton and linen shifts to represent the stars.

39 John Galliano was inspired by Egypt for Christian Dior Spring/Summer 2004 Haute Couture, Paris.

40 Lacroix, sweetie! Jennifer Saunders, Joanna Lumley and Julia Sawalha in *Absolutely Fabulous*, 1996.

41 The Kardashians attend the Kardashian Kollection Launch in Los Angeles, 2011.

42 *Vogue*'s Style Editor-at-Large Princess Elisabeth von Thurn und Taxis (*centre*) at Suno Spring/Summer 2013, New York.

43 Diane von Furstenberg in her iconic leopard-print wrap dress, c.1970s.

44 Princess Grace of Monaco, London, December 1959.

45 Carine Roitfeld, Editor-in-Chief of *CR Book* and former Editor-in-Chief of French *Vogue*, at London Fashion Week, 2010.

46 Veruschka, German countess and model, in a leopard-print bikini for *Vogue*, 1970. Photograph by Franco Rubartelli.

48 Irish McCalla in *Sheena: Queen of the Jungle*, c.1955. McCalla remarked of her role, 'I couldn't act, but I could swing through the trees.'

Primal

'Animals fascinate me because you can find a force, an energy, a fear that also exists in sex.'

Alexander McQueen (1969–2010), fashion designer

The leopard arouses a perfect storm of animal instinct and passion. Psychologists say that our susceptibility is hardwired, a primal response that started with our prehistoric ancestors. Once, the sighting of the pattern of spots on a predator such as a leopard would trigger an instinctive fear. Today that has morphed into attraction and desire. The paradox was encapsulated in the animated American Stone Age sitcom *The Flintstones*, first broadcast in 1960. It was, however, hardly new; the look had been mined since 1918 in the numerous Tarzan movies, which unleashed a rich seam of inspiration for costume designers and glossy magazines. In the 1960s and 70s Veruschka, the German aristo and first supermodel, spearheaded a 'new' mood of primitive, feral power. Six feet of lithe, feline grace, she was a *Vogue* favourite and a natural for savage-chic editorials. American *Vogue* revisited the concept of 'primitive' chic with the Met Costume Institute's exhibition 'Wild: Fashion Untamed' (2004), which examined the use of animal print – most notably leopard – to evoke hyper-sexualized pin-ups.

49 Actress Acquanetta as the High Priestess in *Tarzan and the Leopard Woman*, 1946.

50 Blumarine Spring/Summer 2011, Milan.

51 Adriana Lima for Marc Jacobs Spring/ Summer 2017, New York.

52 Elizabeth Taylor in a publicity still for MGM, 1954.

53 Halle Berry as Miss Stone in the 1994 remake of *The Flintstones*.

54 Veruschka in a floor-length leopard-print dress by Galanos for *Vogue,* June 1965. Photograph by Henry Clarke.

55 Veronica Webb in an Yves Saint
Laurent leopard-print dress.

56 Bacchus, Roman God of Wine,
by Simeon Solomon, 1867.

57 Christian Dior Spring/Summer
2008, Paris.

58 An embroidered leopard pelt

by famed French house Lesage, for Jean
Paul Gaultier Autumn/Winter 1998 Haute
Couture, Paris.

60 Hollywood star Bebe Daniels and her
essential accessory, a pet leopard, 1928.

61 A dog's life: a poodle in a leopard-print
fur coat, 1957.

Pets and Pelts

'Leopards on the gable-ends, leopards on the painted stair … leopards everywhere.'

Vita Sackville-West (1892–1962), writer

The leopard's relationship with humankind is a tragedy of epic proportions. Killed for its skin, kept captive in royal menageries and palaces, a victim of trophy-hunters, the leopard is now endangered in many countries and extinct in others. In the days of the Mughals and maharajahs, Indian royalty kept 'hunting leopards' to bring down gazelles, and Kublai Khan hunted on horseback with his tame leopard riding pillion. From the twelfth and thirteenth centuries onwards, menageries were an exotic attraction in Europe's royal courts. King John of England was said to have a leopard in his menagerie at the Tower of London. The early twentieth century brought a renewed craze for 'pet' leopards as the ultimate accessory. Josephine Baker appeared on stage in Paris with one in the 1920s, and Hollywood stars such as Bebe Daniels, Katharine Hepburn and Gene Tierney posed with real leopards, often wearing leopard-skin themselves.

62 Ralph Lauren Autumn/Winter 2008,
New York.

63 Katharine Hepburn and the titular
'Baby' on the set of *Bringing Up Baby*,
1938. Despite the lure of leopard, the
film lost RKO Pictures US$300,000.

64 Cary Grant, another pet, in *Bringing up Baby*, 1938.

65 French singer, dancer and actress Gaby Deslys, one of the most famous performers of the early 1900s. King Manuel II of Portugal reportedly gave her a necklace worth US$70,000.

67 Actress Gene Tierney in a leopard-print swimsuit with a leopard, 1954.

68–9 The rule-breaking and boundary-pushing French writer, actress and dancer Colette, 1909.

70 Dolce & Gabbana Autumn/Winter 2018, Milan.

71 'L' stands for 'Leopard' in the *Alphabet* suite by artist Erté, c.1976–1977.

72 Barbra Streisand, in a costume by Irene Sharaff, as Fanny Brice in *Funny Girl*, 1968. Streisand's performance won her the 1968 Academy Award for Best Actress.

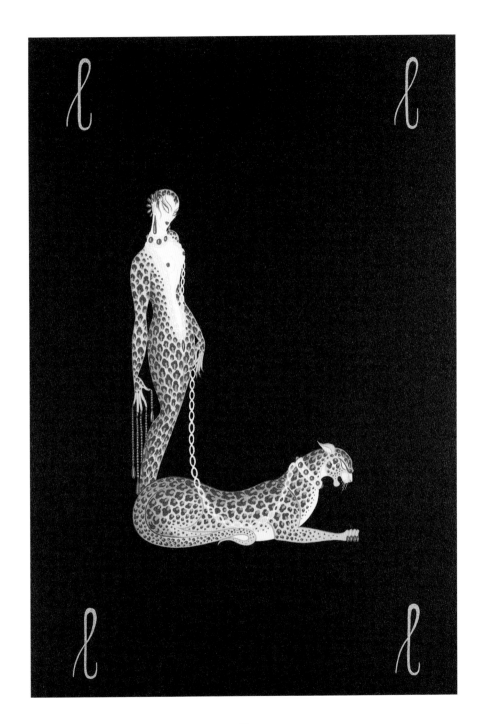

Hollywood

*'My weakness is wearing
too much leopard-print.'*

Jackie Collins (1937–2015), novelist

Leopard has always been catnip to Hollywood,
which revels in its exotic luxe and glamour.
Barbra Streisand is just one of a silver screen
cast of thousands to have been seduced by the
print. In *Funny Girl* (1968) she was dressed by
Irene Sharaff, who also did Elizabeth Taylor's
costumes in *Cleopatra* (1963). However, leopard
had graced the screen as far back as 1917, when
the opera singer and actress Geraldine Farrar
played a leopard-skin-clad Aztec princess in
Cecil B. DeMille's silent *The Woman God Forgot.*
Leopard-print has inspired costume designers
ever since. Hollywood movie goddesses such as
Jean Harlow, Joan Crawford and Rita Hayworth
were dressed by the likes of Adrian, Travis
Banton and Orry-Kelly. Robert Kalloch designed
Carole Lombard's leopard looks in *Twentieth
Century* (1934), and Edith Head and Hubert de
Givenchy dressed Audrey Hepburn in *Charade*
(1963). No pin-up was worth a roll of celluloid
unless she posed in or on leopard-print: just look
at the endless publicity shots of Zsa Zsa Gabor,
Elizabeth Taylor and Marilyn Monroe, among
others. Even Miss Piggy has worn the cult print.

74 Madonna at the MTV Pyjama Party, New York, 1995.

75 Bette Davis in *The Rich Are Always With Us*, 1932.

76 Actress Mary Damon in a leopard-print dress by Adrian, 1949.

77 Jean Harlow, sex-symbol of the 1930s, in *Iron Man,* 1931.

78–9 Frank Gorshin, Cesar Romero, Lee Meriwether and Burgess Meredith star as the Riddler, the Joker, Catwoman and the Penguin in the 1966 version of *Batman*.

80 Carole Lombard on set of comedy classic *Twentieth Century*, 1934.

81 American opera singer and actress Geraldine Farrar, 1917. Her large, slightly fanatical fan-base were nicknamed the 'Gerry-flappers'.

82 Blonde bombshell Jayne Mansfield in leopard-print swimwear, c.1960s.

83 Audrey Hepburn in the pillbox hat extravaganza *Charade*, 1963.

84 Michelle Williams at Louis Vuitton Spring/Summer 2018, Paris.

85 American actor, writer and director Greta Gerwig at the 2015 Sundance Film Festival.

86 Actress and socialite Zsa Zsa Gabor in a leopard-print hat and coat, 1965.

87 The ultimate seal of leopard approval: Miss Piggy in *The Muppets*, 2011.

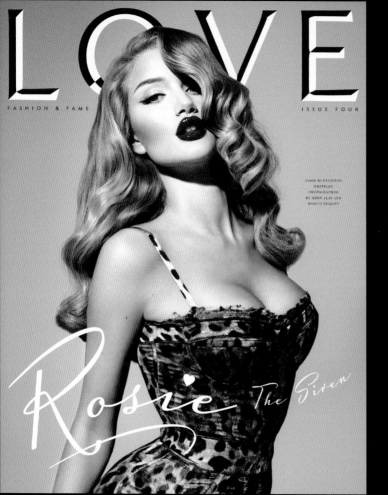

LOVE

FASHION & FAME

ISSUE FOUR

ROSIE HUNTINGTON
WHITELEY
PHOTOGRAPHED
BY MERT ALAS AND
MARCUS PIGGOTT

Rosie *The Siren*

Diva Skin

'As far as I'm concerned, leopard-print is a neutral.'

Jenna Lyons, fashion designer

Leopard-print has sometimes been compared to camouflage, because the leopard is a mistress of disguise in the wild. Conversely, camouflage is the last thing the twenty-first-century 'cat woman' wants. Leopard-print is a powerful fashion statement; it positively roars 'look at me'. Witness the rapper and singer Nicki Minaj arriving at the 2011 Grammy Awards in leopard-print from head to toe, in a Givenchy bodysuit, boots and wig-hat; 'Scary Spice', Mel B, in one of her signature plunge-front leopard-print costumes; or Lady Gaga flouting Maxim's dress code in a see-through leopard-print bodysuit. Whether straight off the catwalks of Givenchy, Cavalli and YSL, or custom-made in skintight Spandex and sequins, leopard-print is the must-have for glamazons and divas alike. From the model-actress Rosie Huntington-Whiteley on the cover of *Love* magazine in leopard-print Dolce & Gabbana to 1950s pin-ups such as Bettie Page, and superstars like Beyoncé and Naomi Campbell, we're never short of mentors in the art of the leopard-print pout and pose.

88 Rosie Huntington-Whiteley in Dolce & Gabbana on the cover of *Love* magazine, September 2010. Photograph by Mert Alas and Marcus Piggott.

90 Pin-up perfection: Ava Gardner, 1952.

91 Nicki Minaj at the 53rd Annual Grammy Awards, Los Angeles, California, 2011.

92 Arielle Dombasle, photographed by Émilie Régnier for her 'Leopard' series, Paris, 2016.

93 Charlotte Dellal at London Fashion Week, 2015.

94—5 Bettie Page often made her own leopard-print bikinis. Here she poses alongside cheetahs in 1954.

96 Kylie Minogue in Dolce & Gabbana on 'Jools Holland's Hootenanny' in London, 2010.

97 The Spice Girls perform in *Spiceworld: The Movie,* 1997.

98 Miss Switzerland contestants in leopard one-pieces in Berne, Switzerland, 1969.

99 Beyoncé headlining in neon leopard-print by Emilio Pucci at the V Festival, England, 2013.

100 Maria Grazia Chiuri for Christian Dior Spring/Summer 2018, Paris.

101 Rita Ora at the V Festival, England, 2014.

102 Scary Spice, Mel B, in a leopard-print catsuit at the Brit Awards, London, 1997.

103 Dancer and actress Cyd Charisse, of *Singin' in the Rain* (1952) fame, in 1955.

104 Gigi Hadid for Max Mara Autumn/ Winter 2018, Milan.

105 Suzy Parker, the inspiration for Audrey Hepburn's role in *Funny Face* (1957), on the cover of *LIFE* magazine, 1951.

106 Taylor Swift, New York, 2016.

107 Lady Gaga at Maxim's for Nicola Formichetti's Thierry Mugler debut, Paris, 2011.

108 Linda Evangelista for Versace Spring/Summer 1992, Milan.

Catwalk

'Leopard makes its way into almost all my collections … I can't seem to be without it.'

Charlotte Olympia Dellal, footwear designer

In the early years of the twentieth century, Paris couturiers such as Jeanne Paquin and Jean-Charles Worth made much use of leopard fur and leopard-print. Inspired by his muse Mitzah Bricard, who wore a leopard-print scarf around her wrist, Christian Dior used the spot in his 1947 'New Look' collection. Pierre Balmain followed in the 1950s, and a young Yves Saint Laurent astounded Paris in 1967 with his 'Africa' collection. Diane von Furstenberg launched a leopard-print wrap dress in 1973. Other major designers, including Gianni Versace, Azzedine Alaïa, Dolce & Gabbana, Anna Molinari, Jean Paul Gaultier, Giorgio Armani, Roberto Cavalli, Marc Jacobs and Alexander McQueen have all gone wild, unleashing leopard-print as a catwalk statement. John Galliano's haute couture Egyptian extravaganza for Dior in January 2004 was an epic of DeMille proportions, with models as fantastical Nefertiti-Hatshepsut hybrids. Encouraged by designer endorsement, the mass market was quick to pounce, turning leopard-print into a timeless, ageless, classless classic, as ubiquitous as denim, stretch or beige.

10 Paul Rückmar & Co advertisement by Carl Moos, Zurich, 1910.

11 John Galliano referencing Christian Dior's iconic muse Mitzah Bricard for Christian Dior Spring/Summer 2008 Haute Couture, Paris.

12 Edie Campbell for Bottega Veneta Spring/Summer 2016, Milan.

113 Christy Turlington for Azzedine Alaïa Autumn/Winter 1991, Milan.

114 'The Jungle Dress' by Christian Dior at his debut 'New Look' collection, Paris, 1947.

115 Christian Dior Autumn/Winter
2009 Haute Couture, Paris.

116–17 Yves Saint Laurent, then Christian
Dior's Artistic Director, at a rehearsal for
the couture house's winter presentation at
Blenheim Palace, United Kingdom, 1958.

118 Tom Ford Autumn/Winter 2018,
New York.

119 Giambattista Valli Autumn/Winter
2011 Haute Couture, Paris.

120 Jean Paul Gaultier Autumn/Winter 2013 Haute Couture, Paris.

121 Gigi Hadid for Jeremy Scott Autumn/ Winter 2017, New York.

122–3 Norbert Schmitt Corps de Ballet in fur coats by Dior, 1969.

124 Dries Van Noten Autumn/Winter 2016, Paris.

125 John Galliano for Christian Dior Autumn/Winter 2004, Paris.

126 Leopard evening dress by Balmain, 1954, Paris.

127 Jean Paul Gaultier Autumn/Winter 2013 Haute Couture, Paris.

On the Prowl

'Isn't every woman's dream to be a feline? In a leopard-print you feel agile and sexy.'

Diane von Furstenberg, fashion designer

Leopard-print is inextricably entwined with sex appeal, representing the perfect marriage of feline and femme fatale. The mood of girls on the prowl was captured in Alexander McQueen's 1997/98 ready-to-wear show for Givenchy in Paris, fittingly titled 'It's a Jungle Out There'. Supermodels stalked the cobbles of an ancient market in the Marais district in leopard-print clothing and boots. Jennifer Lopez was the epitome of feline splendour as she prowled along the red carpet at the Met Ball in 2013 in a Michael Kors leopard-sequinned gown. Joan Crawford, the last of the great movie 'queens', was a fur-coat fanatic, who loved anything leopard and once sent a leopard-skin couch to an MGM press agent as a Christmas present. Leopard woman was a favourite Hollywood motif, leading to several silents – one, by Cecil B. DeMille in 1917, starring the notorious and exotic vamp Louise Glaum. Anne Bancroft, as the ultimate screen cougar, Mrs Robinson, even succeeded in elevating leopard-print lingerie from glamour-mag cliché to upmarket lust-have in *The Graduate* (1967).

128–9 Ungaro Autumn/Winter 1996, Paris.

130 Alexander McQueen for Givenchy Autumn/Winter 1997, Paris.

132 Jennifer Lopez at the Costume Institute Gala for the 'PUNK: Chaos to Couture' exhibition at the Metropolitan Museum of Art, New York, 2013.

133 Screen legend Joan Crawford, photographed by George Hoyningen-Huene in Paris, 1955.

134–5 Grace Jones photographed by Francis Ing for Italian *Playboy* magazine, 1978.

136 Louise Glaum, one of the silent screen's most infamous and exotic vamps, in the silent film *The Leopard Woman* (1920) by Wesley Ruggles.

137 Moschino Cheap and Chic Autumn/
Winter 2010, Milan.

138 Jayne Mansfield at the premiere of
her signature film *Will Success Spoil Rock
Hunter?*, 1957.

139 1960s 'It Girl' and Rolling Stones' muse
Anita Pallenberg in leopard-print body paint
on the set of *Barbarella*, 1968.

140 Kim Kardashian, Halloween, New York, 2010.

141 Kanye West attends Vivienne Westwood Autumn/Winter 2012, Paris.

142 Dustin Hoffman and Anne Bancroft in *The Graduate,* 1967. An instant hit, it was the highest grossing film of 1968 and received seven Oscar nominations.

143 Diamonds – and leopard – are a girl's best friend: Tommy Noonan and Marilyn Monroe in the musical comedy *Gentlemen Prefer Blondes*, 1953.

Wild Things

'My mother thought that anybody who wore leopard was rather vulgar … so naturally I automatically loved it!'

Stephen Jones OBE, milliner

Musicians and the leopard have a magnetic relationship. Well before Rod Stewart, Keith Richards, Steve Tyler, Prince and his leopard-print guitars, Iggy Pop, Kurt Cobain and all the other wild men of rock 'n' roll and punk, swing's elder statesmen of the 1940s and 50s were rocking it. 'Jungle Nights' at New York's Cotton Club featured leopard-skin-clad dancers, and the Rat Pack hung out at the Leopard Lounge in Palm Springs. Leopard-print expressed everything that was anti-establishment, wild, savage, in-your-face and anarchic – a compelling prescription. It was easily subsumed into the punk, glam rock and heavy metal cultures, becoming de rigueur for bands such as T. Rex, the Sex Pistols, the Manic Street Preachers and Roxy Music. And it was a no-brainer dress code for style rebels and originals such as Madonna, Debbie Harry, Alison Mosshart and the late Amy Winehouse, not to mention rock-chick supreme Kate Moss, and the endless entourage of young claimants to her crown.

144 Marc Bolan, lead singer of T. Rex, performing in *Born to Boogie*, 1972.

146 Kate Moss in Covent Garden, London, 2009.

147 Blondie's Debbie Harry, a pioneer of punk rock style in the 1970s and 80s, in 1979.

148 Wild man of rock and animal-print fan Rod Stewart, in cheetah, 1973.

149 Kaia Gerber in leopard-print trousers, Milan Fashion Week, 2017.

150 Prince with leopard-print guitar and strap, performing at the Pepsi Super Bowl halftime show, Miami, 2007.

151 Daisy Lowe for Vivienne Westwood Red Label Spring/Summer 2011, London.

152 Steve Tyler and Aerosmith in 1976.

153 Andy Warhol's Superstar and 1965's 'Girl of the Year', Edie Sedgwick. Photobooth series by Andy Warhol, 1966.

154 Notorious Sex Pistol Sid Vicious and his girlfriend Nancy, played by Gary Oldman and Chloe Webb in the movie *Sid and Nancy*, 1986.

155 Wild thing Keith Richards playing with the Rolling Stones at Candlestick Park, San Francisco, 1981.

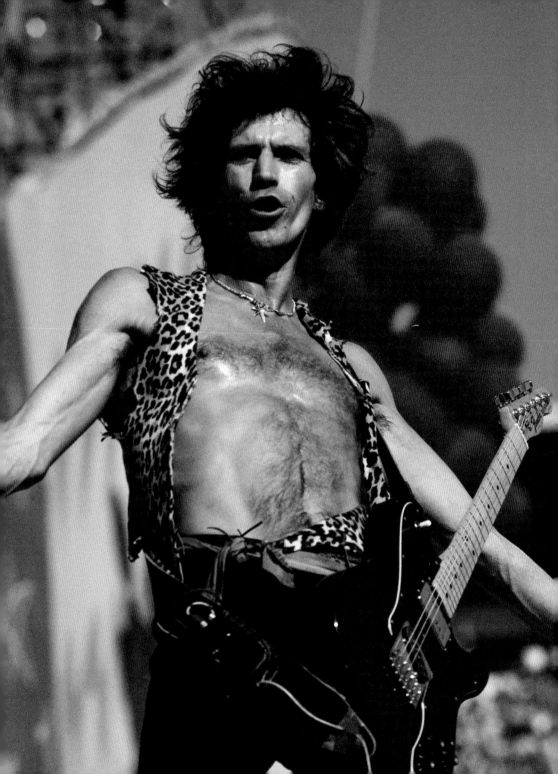

156 Roxy Music's Andy Mackay, Paul Thompson, Bryan Ferry, Brian Eno, Phil Manzanera and Rik Kenton at the Royal College of Art, London, 1972.

157 Sofia Richie at Oscar de la Renta Spring/Summer 2018, New York.

158 The Kill's Alison Mosshart on stage at the V Festival, Melbourne, 2009.

159 Dolce & Gabbana Spring/Summer 2005, Milan.

Animals at Home

'In each of my homes, I have a leopard-print room.'

Ivana Trump, businesswoman

The twentieth-century society decorator Elsie de Wolfe, Lady Mendl, believed that leopard-print was something of an 'avant-garde necessity', and is said to have 'invented' the modern print, when using the real thing for her schemes became prohibitively expensive. The thrill of creating an indoor 'lair' has long excited celebrities. Furniture, wallpaper, bedlinen, lampshades, curtains, clocks, china, crockery and carpets are all available for the star with the hunter in his or her soul – along with leopard-print garden hoses to water the private jungles of the green-fingered. A craze for posing in or sprawling on leopard skins was pioneered by the actresses Gaby Deslys and Claudette Colbert, and echoed in 1970s images of a young Twiggy and a scarcely recognizable, titian-haired Joanna Lumley. The interior designer, writer and cabaret singer Nicky Haslam decorated his study at Eton with leopard-print walls. It should be no surprise to find leopard-print decorating the homes of feline enthusiasts as diverse as Carmen Miranda, Diana Vreeland, Jackie Collins, Valentino and Liam Gallagher.

160 Twiggy on a leopard-skin bed at Biba's
Kensington store, London, 1971.

163 Carmen Miranda had the den in her Hollywood home decorated to match her signature leopard-print bathing suits, California, 1948.

165 Surrealist Salvador Dalí, famed for his sartorial flair, at his home in Cadaqués, Spain.

166 Jackie Collins at home. A collection
of Jackie's leopard-print clothing and
accessories were auctioned at Bonhams,
Los Angeles, in 2017.

167 Elsa Schiaparelli, 1952.

ABBANA

Accessories

'I wore a pair of leopard-print kitten heels to a Conservative Party Conference ... the papers have continued to focus on my feet ever since.'

Theresa May, British Prime Minister

Whether worn on hands, head or feet, wrapped around waists or necks, painted on nails or dyed into buzz cuts, designers and stylists have found a way to use leopard-print in every form of accessory. Leopard-print pillbox hats were a style statement notably associated with Jackie Kennedy and Audrey Hepburn in the 1960s, and it is believed that Bob Dylan's 'Leopard-Skin Pill-Box Hat' (from his album *Blonde on Blonde*, 1966) was inspired by Andy Warhol's muse, the actress Edie Sedgwick. Today's fashionistas and style icons are more likely to go for a top hat by Philip Treacy or Stephen Jones, tote a bag by Givenchy, Dolce & Gabbana or Topshop, or favour leopard-print footwear: booties by Vivienne Westwood or Dior; shoes by Manolo Blahnik or Charlotte Olympia. So, whether you are channelling your inner rock god or prime minister, leopard remains cult, classic, classy and classless – a pin-up in its own right.

170 At the home of French poet, artist, playwright and film-maker Jean Cocteau, Milly-la-Forêt, France.

171 Diana Vreeland at her home in New York, 1976.

172 June Pickney in a leopard fur coat and huge leopard fur-rimmed sunglasses for *LIFE* magazine, 1960.

174 British politician Theresa May at the Conservative Party Conference in Manchester, 2011.

175 Gisele Bündchen photographed by Steven Meisel for the Versace Spring/ Summer 2018 campaign. Artistic Director: Donatella Versace; Art Director: Ferdinando Verderi; Stylist: Jacob K; Make-up: Pat McGrath; Hair: Guido Palau.

176 Jean Paul Gaultier Autumn/Winter 2013, Paris.

177 Vivienne Westwood Spring/Summer 2014, Paris.

178 Sophia Loren wears a leopard-print hat in an airport lounge, 1965.

179 Grace Jones at a rehearsal for 'Pavarotti and Friends' in Modena, Italy, 2002.

180 A guest wears a leopard-inspired bracelet to attend New York Fashion Week, Spring/Summer 2014.

181 Lady Gaga in a leopard collaboration with Agent Provocateur, featuring a Charlotte Olympia beret, styled by Tom Eerebout.

182 Green with envy: a detail from Tom Ford Autumn/Winter 2018, New York.

183 Laced leopard bootees and matching coat by Christian Dior, 1961.

184 Blumarine Autumn/Winter 2008, Milan.

185 A model wearing a suit by Handmacher, hat by Sally Victor and turquoise-spattered jewellery by David Webb, carries a leopard-print handbag. Photograph by Karen Radkai for American *Vogue*, August 1958.

VOGUE

60c

OCTOBER 1

How to spend your clothes-money

"No Regrets"
By Victoria Lincoln

186 American *Vogue*'s 'Winter Fashions' issue, 1914.

187 A still-life of three leopard-patterned handbags, all by Nettie Rosenstein, with Tiffany jewels. Photographed by Richard Rutledge for American *Vogue*, October 1958.

188 Annabel Rosendahl at Paris Fashion Week, Autumn/Winter 2017.

189 Givenchy Autumn/Winter 2007 Haute Couture, Paris.

190 Josephine Baker at the Casino de Paris by Zig, c.1900s.

CASINO DE PARIS

ZIG
30

Picture Credits

Want to learn more about much-needed leopard conservation efforts? Visit:

African Wildlife Foundation:
www.awf.org/wildlife-conservation/leopard

CITES: www.cites.org/

Wildlife Conservation Society: www.wcs.org

World Wildlife Fund: www.worldwildlife.org

LAURENCE KING

Published in 2018
by Laurence King Publishing Ltd
361–373 City Road
London EC1V 1LR
United Kingdom
Tel: +44 20 7841 6900
Fax: +44 20 7841 6910
E-mail: enquiries@laurenceking.com
www.laurenceking.com

A catalogue record for this book is available
from the British Library

ISBN: 978-1-78627-324-6

Senior commissioning editor: Camilla Morton
Editor: Katherine Pitt
Picture researcher: Giulia Hetherington
Design: Stuart Dando

Front cover: Claudia Schiffer in Christian Dior.
Photograph by Liz Collins for *Numero TOKYO*,
April 2009 © Liz Collins/Trunk Archive
Leopard pattern © EcoPrint/Shutterstock

Printed in Italy